CELLO

101 MOST BEAUTIFUL SONGS

CW00539453

Available for
FLUTE, CLARINET, ALTO SAX, TENOR SAX, TRUMPET,
HORN, TROMBONE, VIOLIN, VIOLA, CELLO

ISBN 978-1-5400-4828-8

For all works contained herein:
Unauthorized copying, arranging, adapting, recording, Internet posting, public performance,
or other distribution of the music in this publication is an infringement of copyright.
Infringers are liable under the law.

Visit Hal Leonard Online at
www.halleonard.com

Contact us:
Hal Leonard
7777 West Bluemound Road
Milwaukee, WI 53213
Email: info@halleonard.com

In Europe, contact:
Hal Leonard Europe Limited
42 Wigmore Street
Marylebone, London, W1U 2RN
Email: info@halleonardeurope.com

In Australia, contact:
Hal Leonard Australia Pty. Ltd.
4 Lentara Court
Cheltenham, Victoria, 3192 Australia
Email: info@halleonard.com.au

CONTENTS

ALWAYS

CELLO

Words and Music by
IRVING BERLIN

Moderate Waltz

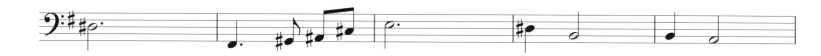

© Copyright 1925 by Irving Berlin
Copyright Renewed
International Copyright Secured   All Rights Reserved

ALWAYS ON MY MIND

CELLO

Words and Music by WAYNE THOMPSON,
MARK JAMES and JOHNNY CHRISTOPHER

Copyright © 1971 Screen Gems-EMI Music Inc.
Copyright Renewed
All Rights Administered by Sony/ATV Music Publishing LLC, 424 Church Street, Suite 1200, Nashville, TN 37219
International Copyright Secured   All Rights Reserved

AND I LOVE HER

CELLO

Words and Music by JOHN LENNON
and PAUL McCARTNEY

Copyright © 1964 Sony/ATV Music Publishing LLC
Copyright Renewed
All Rights Administered by Sony/ATV Music Publishing LLC, 424 Church Street, Suite 1200, Nashville, TN 37219
International Copyright Secured   All Rights Reserved

AND I LOVE YOU SO

CELLO

Words and Music by
DON McLEAN

Copyright © 1970, 1972 BENNY BIRD CO., INC.
Copyright Renewed
All Rights Controlled and Administered by SONGS OF UNIVERSAL, INC.
All Rights Reserved   Used by Permission

AND SO IT GOES

CELLO

Words and Music by
BILLY JOEL

Slow Ballad, with much rubato

Copyright © 1989 JOELSONGS
All Rights Administered by ALMO MUSIC CORP.
All Rights Reserved   Used by Permission

ANNIE'S SONG

CELLO

Words and Music by
JOHN DENVER

Copyright © 1974 My Pop's Songs, Dino Park Publishing and JD Legacy Publishing
Copyright Renewed
All Rights Administered by Kobalt Songs Music Publishing
All Rights Reserved   Used by Permission

ANYWHERE IS

CELLO

Words and Music by ENYA,
NICKY RYAN and ROMA RYAN

Copyright © 1995 EMI Music Publishing Ltd.
All Rights Administered by Sony/ATV Music Publishing LLC, 424 Church Street, Suite 1200, Nashville, TN 37219
International Copyright Secured   All Rights Reserved

BEIN' GREEN

CELLO

Words and Music by
JOE RAPOSO

Slowly, reflectively

Copyright © 1970 by Jonico Music, Inc.
Copyright Renewed
All Rights in the U.S.A. Administered by Green Fox Music, Inc.
International Copyright Secured   All Rights Reserved

BLACKBIRD

CELLO

Words and Music by JOHN LENNON
and PAUL McCARTNEY

Copyright © 1968, 1969 Sony/ATV Music Publishing LLC
Copyright Renewed
All Rights Administered by Sony/ATV Music Publishing LLC, 424 Church Street, Suite 1200, Nashville, TN 37219
International Copyright Secured   All Rights Reserved

THE BOOK OF LOVE

CELLO

Words and Music by
STEPHIN MERRITT

© 1999 Stephin Merritt
Published by Gay & Loud (ASCAP)
All Rights Reserved   Used by Permission

CODA

THE BOXER

CELLO

Words and Music by
PAUL SIMON

Copyright © 1968 Paul Simon (BMI)
International Copyright Secured All Rights Reserved
Used by Permission

BRING HIM HOME

from LES MISÉRABLES

Cello

Music by CLAUDE-MICHEL SCHÖNBERG
Lyrics by HERBERT KRETZMER and ALAIN BOUBLIL

small notes optional

Music and English Lyrics Copyright © 1986 by Alain Boublil Music Ltd. (ASCAP)
French Lyrics Copyright © 1991 by Editions Musicales Alain Boublil
Mechanical and Publication Rights for the U.S.A. Administered by Alain Boublil Music Ltd. (ASCAP) c/o Spielman Koenigsberg & Parker LLP,
Richard Koenigsberg, 1675 Broadway, 20th Floor, New York NY 10019, Tel 212-453-2500, Fax 212-453-2550, ABML@skpny.com
International Copyright Secured. All Rights Reserved. This music is copyright. Photocopying is illegal.
All Performance Rights Restricted.

BY THE TIME I GET TO PHOENIX

CELLO

Words and Music by
JIMMY WEBB

Copyright © 1967 R2M Music, Songs Of Lastrada and EMI Sosaha Music Inc.
Copyright Renewed
All Rights for R2M Music and Songs Of Lastrada Administered by BMG Rights Management (US) LLC
All Rights for EMI Sosaha Music Inc. Administered by Sony/ATV Music Publishing LLC, 424 Church Street, Suite 1200, Nashville, TN 37219
All Rights Reserved   Used by Permission

CANDLE IN THE WIND

Cello

Words and Music by ELTON JOHN
and BERNIE TAUPIN

Copyright © 1973 UNIVERSAL/DICK JAMES MUSIC LTD.
Copyright Renewed
All Rights in the United States and Canada Controlled and Administered by UNIVERSAL - SONGS OF POLYGRAM INTERNATIONAL, INC.
All Rights Reserved   Used by Permission

A CHILD IS BORN

CELLO

By THAD JONES

Copyright © 1969 D'Accord Music, c/o Publishers' Licensing Corporation, 48 South Park Street, Unit 615, Montclair, NJ 07042-2788
Copyright Renewed
All Rights Reserved

(They Long to Be)
CLOSE TO YOU

CELLO

Lyrics by HAL DAVID
Music by BURT BACHARACH

Copyright © 1963 BMG Rights Management (UK) Ltd. and New Hidden Valley Music Co.
Copyright Renewed
All Rights Administered by BMG Rights Management (US) LLC
All Rights Reserved   Used by Permission

CITY OF STARS
from LA LA LAND

CELLO

Music by JUSTIN HURWITZ
Lyrics by BENJ PASEK & JUSTIN PAUL

© 2016 Justin Hurwitz Music (BMI), Warner-Tamerlane Publishing Corp. (BMI), administered by Warner-Tamerlane Publishing Corp. (BMI)/
B Lion Music (BMI), administered by Songs Of Universal, Inc. (BMI)/Pick In A Pinch Music (ASCAP), breathelike music (ASCAP),
WB Music Corp. (ASCAP), administered by WB Music Corp. (ASCAP)/A Lion Music (ASCAP), administered by Universal Music Corp. (ASCAP)
All Rights Reserved   Used by Permission

COME SUNDAY
from BLACK, BROWN & BEIGE

CELLO

By DUKE ELLINGTON

Copyright © 1946 (Renewed) by G. Schirmer, Inc. (ASCAP)
International Copyright Secured   All Rights Reserved
Reprinted by Permission

CRAZY

CELLO

Words and Music by
WILLIE NELSON

Copyright © 1961 Sony/ATV Music Publishing LLC
Copyright Renewed
All Rights Administered by Sony/ATV Music Publishing LLC, 424 Church Street, Suite 1200, Nashville, TN 37219
International Copyright Secured   All Rights Reserved

CRYING

CELLO

Words and Music by ROY ORBISON
and JOE MELSON

Moderately slow, with feeling

Copyright © 1961 Sony/ATV Music Publishing LLC, R Key Darkus Publishing, Orbi Lee Publishing, Barbara Orbison Music Company and Roys Boys LLC
Copyright Renewed
All Rights on behalf of Sony/ATV Music Publishing LLC Administered by Sony/ATV Music Publishing LLC, 424 Church Street, Suite 1200, Nashville, TN 37219
All Rights on behalf of R Key Darkus Publishing, Orbi Lee Publishing, Barbara Orbison Music Company and Roys Boys LLC Administered by Songs Of Kobalt Music Publishing
International Copyright Secured   All Rights Reserved

DREAM A LITTLE DREAM OF ME

Cello

Words by GUS KAHN
Music by WILBUR SCHWANDT
and FABIAN ANDREE

TRO - © Copyright 1930 (Renewed) and 1931 (Renewed) Essex Music, Inc., Words and Music, Inc., New York, NY,
Don Swan Publications, Miami, FL and Gilbert Keyes Music, Hollywood, CA
International Copyright Secured
All Rights Reserved Including Public Performance For Profit
Used by Permission

DAUGHTERS

CELLO

Words and Music by
JOHN MAYER

Copyright © 2003 Specific Harm Music
All Rights Administered by Goodium Music, Inc., c/o Cal Financial Group, 700 Harris Street, Suite 201, Charlottesville, VA 22903
International Copyright Secured   All Rights Reserved

EASY LIVING
Theme from the Paramount Picture EASY LIVING

CELLO

Words and Music by LEO ROBIN
and RALPH RAINGER

Copyright © 1937 Sony/ATV Music Publishing LLC
Copyright Renewed
All Rights Administered by Sony/ATV Music Publishing LLC, 424 Church Street, Suite 1200, Nashville, TN 37219
International Copyright Secured   All Rights Reserved

ETERNAL FLAME

CELLO

Words and Music by BILLY STEINBERG,
TOM KELLY and SUSANNA HOFFS

Copyright © 1988 Sony/ATV Music Publishing LLC and Bangophile Music
All Rights on behalf of Sony/ATV Music Publishing LLC Administered by Sony/ATV Music Publishing LLC, 424 Church Street, Suite 1200, Nashville, TN 37219
All Rights on behalf of Bangophile Music Controlled and Administered by Songs Of Universal, Inc.
International Copyright Secured   All Rights Reserved

ETERNALLY

CELLO

Words by GEOFFREY PARSONS
Music by CHARLES CHAPLIN

Slowly, with feeling

Copyright © 1953 by Bourne Co. (ASCAP)
Copyright Renewed
International Copyright Secured All Rights Reserved

EVERY BREATH YOU TAKE

CELLO

Music and Lyrics by
STING

Copyright © 1983 G.M. Sumner
All Rights Administered by Sony/ATV Music Publishing LLC, 424 Church Street, Suite 1200, Nashville, TN 37219
International Copyright Secured   All Rights Reserved

(EVERYTHING I DO) I DO IT FOR YOU

from the Motion Picture ROBIN HOOD: PRINCE OF THIEVES

Cello

Written by MICHAEL KAMEN

Copyright © 1991 Zachary Creek Music, Inc. and J.G. RTISTS, Inc.
All Rights Administered by Kobalt Music Group Ltd.
International Copyright Secured   All Rights Reserved

FEELING GOOD

from THE ROAR OF THE GREASEPAINT – THE SMELL OF THE CROWD

CELLO

Words and Music by LESLIE BRICUSSE
and ANTHONY NEWLEY

© Copyright 1964 (Renewed) Concord Music Ltd., London, England
TRO - Musical Comedy Productions, Inc., New York, controls all publication rights for the U.S.A. and Canada
International Copyright Secured
All Rights Reserved Including Public Performance For Profit
Used by Permission

FOR ALL WE KNOW

CELLO

Words by SAM M. LEWIS
Music by J. FRED COOTS

Copyright © 1934 (Renewed) and 1956 (Renewed) by Sis 'N Bro Music Company, Toy Town Tunes, Inc. and John F. Coots Jr. Trust Music
All Rights for Toy Town Tunes, Inc. and John F. Coots Jr. Trust Music Administered in the United States and Canada by Wixen Music Publishing, Inc.
All Rights for the Sam M. Lewis share in Canada Administered by Redwood Music Ltd.
International Copyright Secured   All Rights Reserved
Used by Permission

GABRIEL'S OBOE

from the Motion Picture THE MISSION

CELLO

Words and Music by
ENNIO MORRICONE

Copyright © 1986 BMG VM Music Ltd.
All Rights Administered by BMG Rights Management (US) LLC
All Rights Reserved   Used by Permission

GOOD NIGHT

CELLO

Words and Music by JOHN LENNON
and PAUL McCARTNEY

Copyright © 1968 Sony/ATV Music Publishing LLC
Copyright Renewed
All Rights Administered by Sony/ATV Music Publishing LLC, 424 Church Street, Suite 1200, Nashville, TN 37219
International Copyright Secured   All Rights Reserved

GOODNIGHT, SWEETHEART, GOODNIGHT

(Goodnight, It's Time to Go)

CELLO

Words and Music by JAMES HUDSON
and CALVIN CARTER

Copyright © 1953, 1954 (Renewed) by Arc Music Corporation (BMI)
Worldwide Rights Owned by Arc/Conrad Music LLC
All Rights Administered by BMG Rights Management (US) LLC
International Copyright Secured   All Rights Reserved
Used by Permission

HAVE I TOLD YOU LATELY

CELLO

Words and Music by
VAN MORRISON

Copyright © 1989 Barrule UK Ltd.
All Rights Administered by BMG Rights Management (US) LLC
All Rights Reserved   Used by Permission

HELLO

CELLO

Words and Music by
LIONEL RICHIE

Copyright © 1983 by Brockman Music and Brenda Richie Publishing
All Rights Reserved   Used by Permission

HEAL THE WORLD

CELLO

Words and Music by
MICHAEL JACKSON

Copyright © 1991 Mijac Music
All Rights Administered by Sony/ATV Music Publishing LLC, 424 Church Street, Suite 1200, Nashville, TN 37219
International Copyright Secured   All Rights Reserved

HERE, THERE AND EVERYWHERE

CELLO

Words and Music by JOHN LENNON
and PAUL McCARTNEY

Copyright © 1966 Sony/ATV Music Publishing LLC
Copyright Renewed
All Rights Administered by Sony/ATV Music Publishing LLC, 424 Church Street, Suite 1200, Nashville, TN 37219
International Copyright Secured   All Rights Reserved

HIGHLAND CATHEDRAL

CELLO

By MICHAEL KORB
and ULRICH ROEVER

Stately March, in 2

Copyright © 1992 EDITION ROMA
All Rights for the Western Hemisphere Controlled and Administered by UNIVERSAL MUSIC CORP.
All Rights Reserved   Used by Permission

I HAVE A DREAM
from MAMMA MIA!

CELLO

Words and Music by BENNY ANDERSSON
and BJÖRN ULVAEUS

Copyright © 1979 UNIVERSAL/UNION SONGS MUSIKFORLAG AB
All Rights in the United States and Canada Controlled and Administered by
UNIVERSAL - POLYGRAM INTERNATIONAL PUBLISHING, INC. and EMI WATERFORD MUSIC, INC.
All Rights Reserved   Used by Permission

I LEFT MY HEART IN SAN FRANCISCO

CELLO

Words by DOUGLASS CROSS
Music by GEORGE CORY

Copyright © 1954 Colgems-EMI Music Inc.
Copyright Renewed
All Rights Administered by Sony/ATV Music Publishing LLC, 424 Church Street, Suite 1200, Nashville, TN 37219
International Copyright Secured   All Rights Reserved

I WILL

CELLO

Words and Music by JOHN LENNON
and PAUL McCARTNEY

Copyright © 1968 Sony/ATV Music Publishing LLC
Copyright Renewed
All Rights Administered by Sony/ATV Music Publishing LLC, 424 Church Street, Suite 1200, Nashville, TN 37219
International Copyright Secured   All Rights Reserved

I'LL BE AROUND

CELLO

Words and Music by
ALEC WILDER

Slowly, with expression

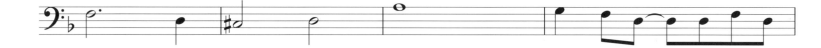

TRO - © Copyright 1942 (Renewed) Ludlow Music, Inc., New York, NY
International Copyright Secured
All Rights Reserved Including Public Performance For Profit
Used by Permission

I'LL BE SEEING YOU

from RIGHT THIS WAY

CELLO

Written by IRVING KAHAL
and SAMMY FAIN

Copyright © 1938 BMG Gold Songs and Fain Music Co.
Copyright Renewed
All Rights for BMG Gold Songs Administered by BMG Rights Management (US) LLC
All Rights in Canada Administered by Redwood Music Ltd. and Williamson Music, a Division of Rodgers & Hammerstein: an Imagem Company
All Rights Reserved   Used by Permission

I'VE DREAMED OF YOU

CELLO

Words and Music by ANN HAMPTON CALLAWAY
and ROLF LOVLAND

© 1999 WB MUSIC CORP., HALARON MUSIC, WORKS OF HEART PUBLISHING, EMANUEL MUSIC CORP. and UNIVERSAL - MCA PUBLISHING SCANDINAVIA
All Rights for HALARON MUSIC, WORKS OF HEART PUBLISHING and EMANUEL MUSIC CORP. Administered by WB MUSIC CORP.
All Rights for UNIVERSAL - MCA PUBLISHING SCANDINAVIA in the U.S. and Canada Controlled and Administered by
UNIVERSAL - MCA MUSIC PUBLISHING, a Division of UNIVERSAL STUDIOS, INC.
All Rights Reserved   Used by Permission

Freely

IN MY ROOM

CELLO

Words and Music by BRIAN WILSON
and GARY USHER

Copyright © 1964 IRVING MUSIC, INC.
Copyright Renewed
All Rights Reserved   Used by Permission

LA VIE EN ROSE
(Take Me to Your Heart Again)

CELLO

Original French Lyrics by EDITH PIAF
Music by LUIGUY
English Lyrics by MACK DAVID

Copyright © 1950 Editions Beuscher Arpege and Universal - PolyGram International Publishing, Inc.
Copyright Renewed
All Rights on behalf of Editions Beuscher Arpege Administered by Sony/ATV Music Publishing LLC, 424 Church Street, Suite 1200, Nashville, TN 37219
International Copyright Secured   All Rights Reserved

JUST GIVE ME A REASON

Cello

Words and Music by ALECIA MOORE,
JEFF BHASKER and NATE RUESS

Copyright © 2012 EMI Blackwood Music Inc., Pink Inside Publishing, Sony/ATV Music Publishing LLC, Way Above Music, WC Music Corp., FBR Music and Bearvon Music
All Rights on behalf of EMI Blackwood Music Inc., Pink Inside Publishing, Sony/ATV Music Publishing LLC
and Way Above Music Administered by Sony/ATV Music Publishing LLC, 424 Church Street, Suite 1200, Nashville, TN 37219
All Rights on behalf of FBR Music and Bearvon Music Administered by WC Music Corp.
International Copyright Secured   All Rights Reserved

CODA

LADY IN RED

CELLO

Words and Music by
CHRIS DeBURGH

Moderately slow

Copyright © 2002 Hornall Brothers Music Ltd.
All Rights Administered by BMG Rights Management (US) LLC
All Rights Reserved   Used by Permission

LET IT BE ME
(Je t'appartiens)

English Words by MANN CURTIS
French Words by PIERRE DeLANOE
Music by GILBERT BECAUD

CELLO

Copyright © 1955, 1957, 1960 FRANCE MUSIC COMPANY
Copyrights Renewed
All Rights for the U.S. and Canada Controlled and Administered by UNIVERSAL MUSIC CORP.
All Rights Reserved   Used by Permission

LOST IN YOUR EYES

CELLO

Words and Music by
DEBORAH GIBSON

Copyright © 1987, 1989 by Music Sales Corporation (ASCAP)
International Copyright Secured   All Rights Reserved
Reprinted by Permission

LOVE ME TENDER

CELLO

Words and Music by ELVIS PRESLEY
and VERA MATSON

Moderately slow

Copyright © 1956; Renewed 1984 Elvis Presley Music (BMI)
All Rights Administered by Songs Of Steve Peter and Songs Of Kobalt Music Publishing
International Copyright Secured   All Rights Reserved

LOVING YOU

CELLO

Words and Music by JERRY LEIBER
and MIKE STOLLER

Copyright © 1957 Sony/ATV Music Publishing LLC
Copyright Renewed
All Rights Administered by Sony/ATV Music Publishing LLC, 424 Church Street, Suite 1200, Nashville, TN 37219
International Copyright Secured   All Rights Reserved

LULLABYE
(Goodnight, My Angel)

CELLO

Words and Music by
BILLY JOEL

Rubato, gently

Copyright © 1993 IMPULSIVE MUSIC
All Rights Administered by ALMO MUSIC CORP.
All Rights Reserved   Used by Permission

MIA & SEBASTIAN'S THEME

from LA LA LAND

CELLO

Music by
JUSTIN HURWITZ

Moderately slow, expressively

© 2016 B Lion Music (BMI) administered by Songs Of Universal, Inc. (BMI)/Warner-Tamerlane Publishing Corp. (BMI)
All Rights Reserved   Used by Permission

MICHELLE

CELLO

Words and Music by JOHN LENNON
and PAUL McCARTNEY

Copyright © 1965 Sony/ATV Music Publishing LLC
Copyright Renewed
All Rights Administered by Sony/ATV Music Publishing LLC, 424 Church Street, Suite 1200, Nashville, TN 37219
International Copyright Secured   All Rights Reserved

MONA LISA

from the Paramount Picture CAPTAIN CAREY, U.S.A.

CELLO

Words and Music by JAY LIVINGSTON
and RAY EVANS

Copyright © 1949 Sony/ATV Music Publishing LLC
Copyright Renewed
All Rights Administered by Sony/ATV Music Publishing LLC, 424 Church Street, Suite 1200, Nashville, TN 37219
International Copyright Secured   All Rights Reserved

MY FOOLISH HEART

CELLO

Words by NED WASHINGTON
Music by VICTOR YOUNG

Slowly and expressively

Copyright © 1949 by Chappell & Co., Inc., Catharine Hinen Music and Patti Washington Music
Copyright Renewed
All Rights for Catharine Hinen Music Administered by Shapiro, Bernstein & Co., Inc.
International Copyright Secured   All Rights Reserved

MY FUNNY VALENTINE

from BABES IN ARMS

Cello

Words by LORENZ HART
Music by RICHARD RODGERS

Copyright © 1937 by Chappell & Co., Inc.
Copyright Renewed
Copyright Assigned to Williamson Music, a Division of Rodgers & Hammerstein: an Imagem Company
and WC Music Corp. for the extended renewal period of copyright in the USA
International Copyright Secured   All Rights Reserved

MY VALENTINE

CELLO

Words and Music by
PAUL McCARTNEY

© 2012 MPL COMMUNICATIONS LTD.
Administered by MPL COMMUNICATIONS, INC.
All Rights Reserved

MY WAY

English Words by PAUL ANKA
Original French Words by GILLES THIBAULT
Music by JACQUES REVAUX and CLAUDE FRANCOIS

CELLO

Copyright © 1967 Societe Des Nouvelles and Editions Eddie Barclay
Copyright © 1969 Chrysalis Standards, Inc. and iWay Holdings SAS
Copyright Renewed
All Rights for Chrysalis Standards, Inc. Administered by BMG Rights Management (US) LLC
All Rights Reserved   Used by Permission

NANCY WITH THE LAUGHING FACE

CELLO

Words by PHIL SILVERS
Music by JAMES VAN HEUSEN

Copyright © 1942 Van Heusen Music Corp. and Barton Music Corp.
Copyright Renewed
All Rights for Van Heusen Music Corp. in the United States Administered by Imagem Sounds
All Rights Reserved   Used by Permission

NATURE BOY

CELLO

Words and Music by
EDEN AHBEZ

Copyright © 1948 by Eden Ahbez
Copyright Renewed 1975 by Golden World
International Copyright Secured   All Rights Reserved

NEVER ENOUGH
from THE GREATEST SHOWMAN

CELLO

Words and Music by BENJ PASEK
and JUSTIN PAUL

Copyright © 2017 Breathelike Music, Pick In A Pinch Music and T C F Music Publishing, Inc.
All Rights for Breathelike Music and Pick In A Pinch Music Administered Worldwide by Kobalt Songs Music Publishing
All Rights Reserved   Used by Permission

A NIGHTINGALE SANG IN BERKELEY SQUARE

CELLO

Lyric by ERIC MASCHWITZ
Music by MANNING SHERWIN

Copyright © 1940 The Peter Maurice Music Co., Ltd., London, England
Copyright Renewed and Assigned to Shapiro, Bernstein & Co., Inc., New York for U.S.A. and Canada
International Copyright Secured   All Rights Reserved
Used by Permission

PERFECT

CELLO

Words and Music by
ED SHEERAN

Copyright © 2017 Sony/ATV Music Publishing (UK) Limited
All Rights Administered by Sony/ATV Music Publishing LLC, 424 Church Street, Suite 1200, Nashville, TN 37219
International Copyright Secured   All Rights Reserved

PHOTOGRAPH

CELLO

Words and Music by ED SHEERAN,
JOHNNY McDAID, MARTIN PETER HARRINGTON
and TOM LEONARD

Copyright © 2014 Sony/ATV Music Publishing (UK) Limited, Spirit B-Unique Polar Patrol, Halosongs and Halomani Songs/Softgrass Songs
All Rights on behalf of Sony/ATV Music Publishing (UK) Limited Administered by Sony/ATV Music Publishing LLC, 424 Church Street, Suite 1200, Nashville, TN 37219
All Rights on behalf of Spirit B-Unique Polar Patrol Controlled and Administered by Spirit B-Unique Polar Patrol Songs
All Rights on behalf of Halosongs and Halomani Songs/Softgrass Songs Controlled and Administered by Songs Of Imagem Music and Imagem Sounds
International Copyright Secured   All Rights Reserved

THE PLACE WHERE LOST THINGS GO

from MARY POPPINS RETURNS

CELLO

Music by MARC SHAIMAN
Lyrics by SCOTT WITTMAN and MARC SHAIMAN

© 2018 Walt Disney Music Company
All Rights Reserved. Used by Permission.

RAINY DAYS AND MONDAYS

CELLO

Lyrics by PAUL WILLIAMS
Music by ROGER NICHOLS

Moderately slow

Copyright © 1970 ALMO MUSIC CORP.
Copyright Renewed
All Rights Reserved   Used by Permission

RELEASE ME

CELLO

Words and Music by ROBERT YOUNT,
EDDIE MILLER and DUB WILLIAMS

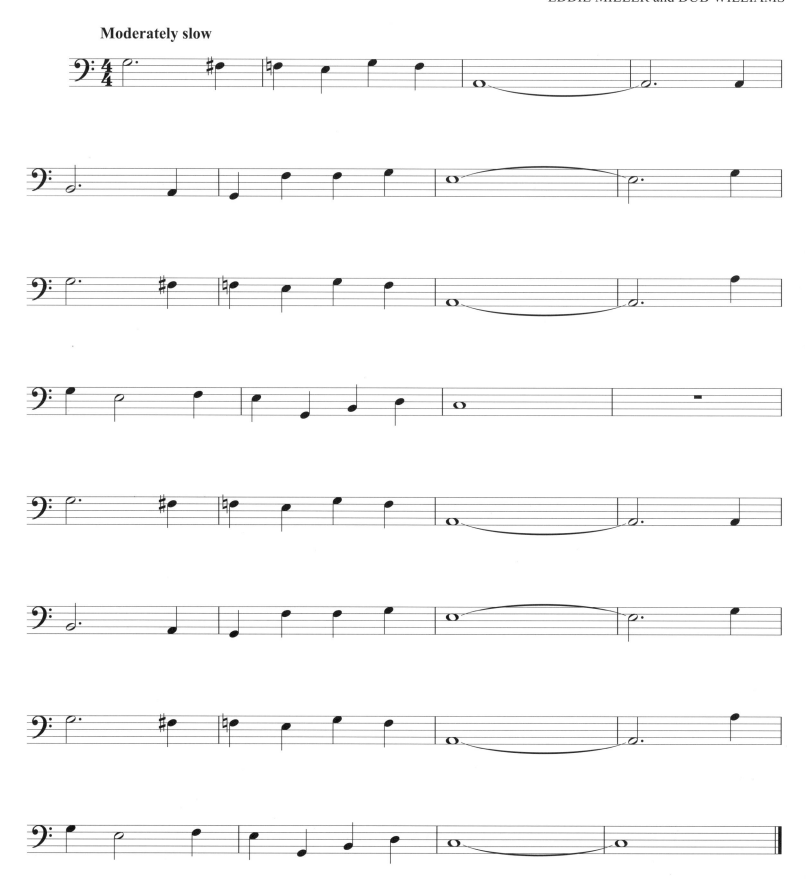

Copyright © 1954 Sony/ATV Music Publishing LLC and Roschelle Publishing in the U.S.A.
Copyright Renewed
All Rights outside the U.S.A. Administered by Sony/ATV Music Publishing LLC
All Rights on behalf of Sony/ATV Music Publishing LLC Administered by Sony/ATV Music Publishing LLC, 424 Church Street, Suite 1200, Nashville, TN 37219
International Copyright Secured   All Rights Reserved

REWRITE THE STARS

from THE GREATEST SHOWMAN

CELLO

Words and Music by BENJ PASEK
and JUSTIN PAUL

Copyright © 2017 Breathelike Music, Pick In A Pinch Music and T C F Music Publishing, Inc.
All Rights for Breathelike Music and Pick In A Pinch Music Administered Worldwide by Kobalt Songs Music Publishing
All Rights Reserved   Used by Permission

RIVER FLOWS IN YOU

CELLO

By YIRUMA

Copyright © 2011 Sony/ATV Music Publishing (Hong Kong Korean Branch)
All Rights Administered by Sony/ATV Music Publishing LLC, 424 Church Street, Suite 1200, Nashville, TN 37219
International Copyright Secured   All Rights Reserved

SCARBOROUGH FAIR/CANTICLE

CELLO

Arrangement and Original Counter Melody by
PAUL SIMON and ARTHUR GARFUNKEL

Copyright © 1966 (Renewed) Paul Simon and Arthur Garfunkel (BMI)
International Copyright Secured All Rights Reserved
Used by Permission

SHALLOW

from A STAR IS BORN

Cello

Words and Music by STEFANI GERMANOTTA,
MARK RONSON, ANDREW WYATT
and ANTHONY ROSSOMANDO

Copyright © 2018 Sony/ATV Music Publishing LLC, House Of Gaga Publishing LLC, Concord Copyrights, Songs Of Zelig,
Downtown DMP Songs, Downtown DLJ Songs, Warner-Barham Music, LLC and Warner-Olive Music, LLC
All Rights on behalf of Sony/ATV Music Publishing LLC and House Of Gaga Publishing LLC Administered by
Sony/ATV Music Publishing LLC, 424 Church Street, Suite 1200, Nashville, TN 37219
All Rights on behalf of Songs Of Zelig Administered by Concord Copyrights
All Rights on behalf of Downtown DMP Songs and Downtown DLJ Songs Administered by Downtown Music Publishing LLC
All Rights (Excluding Print) on behalf of Warner-Barham Music, LLC Administered by Songs Of Universal, Inc.
All Rights (Excluding Print) on behalf of Warner-Olive Music, LLC Administered by Universal Music Corp.
Exclusive Worldwide Print Rights on behalf of Warner-Barham Music, LLC and Warner-Olive Music, LLC Administered by Alfred Music
International Copyright Secured All Rights Reserved

SINCE I DON'T HAVE YOU

Words and Music by JAMES BEAUMONT,
JANET VOGEL, JOSEPH VERSCHAREN,
WALTER LESTER, LENNIE MARTIN,
JOSEPH ROCK and JOHN TAYLOR

Cello

Slowly, with a strong, rockin' beat

Copyright © 1959 by Bonnyview Music Corp.
Copyright Renewed
All Rights Administered by Southern Music Pub. Co. Inc.
International Copyright Secured   All Rights Reserved

SHE'S ALWAYS A WOMAN

CELLO

Words and Music by
BILLY JOEL

Copyright © 1977 IMPULSIVE MUSIC
Copyright Renewed
All Rights Administered by ALMO MUSIC CORP.
All Rights Reserved   Used by Permission

SMILE
Theme from MODERN TIMES

CELLO

Words by JOHN TURNER and GEOFFREY PARSONS
Music by CHARLES CHAPLIN

Moderately, with great warmth

Copyright © 1954 by Bourne Co. (ASCAP)
Copyright Renewed
International Copyright Secured   All Rights Reserved

SMOKE GETS IN YOUR EYES

from ROBERTA

CELLO

Words by OTTO HARBACH
Music by JEROME KERN

Copyright © 1933 UNIVERSAL - POLYGRAM INTERNATIONAL PUBLISHING, INC.
Copyright Renewed
All Rights Reserved   Used by Permission

SOMETHING WONDERFUL
from THE KING AND I

CELLO

Lyrics by OSCAR HAMMERSTEIN II
Music by RICHARD RODGERS

Copyright © 1951 by Richard Rodgers and Oscar Hammerstein II
Copyright Renewed
Williamson Music, a Division of Rodgers & Hammerstein: an Imagem Company, owner of publication and allied rights throughout the world
International Copyright Secured   All Rights Reserved

SOMEWHERE

from WEST SIDE STORY

Cello

Lyrics by STEPHEN SONDHEIM
Music by LEONARD BERNSTEIN

Copyright © 1957 by Amberson Holdings LLC and Stephen Sondheim
Copyright Renewed
Leonard Bernstein Music Publishing Company LLC, Publisher
Boosey & Hawkes, Inc., Sole Agent
Copyright for All Countries All Rights Reserved

THE SOUND OF SILENCE

CELLO

Words and Music by
PAUL SIMON

Copyright © 1964 Paul Simon (BMI)
International Copyright Secured   All Rights Reserved
Used by Permission

STARDUST

Words by MITCHELL PARISH
Music by HOAGY CARMICHAEL

CELLO

Copyright © 1928, 1929 by Songs Of Peer, Ltd. and EMI Mills Music, Inc.
Copyrights Renewed
All Rights outside the USA Controlled by EMI Mills Music, Inc. (Publishing) and Alfred Music (Print)
International Copyright Secured   All Rights Reserved

STRANGERS IN THE NIGHT

adapted from A MAN COULD GET KILLED

Cello

Words by CHARLES SINGLETON
and EDDIE SNYDER
Music by BERT KAEMPFERT

Moderately slow

Copyright © 1966 SONGS OF UNIVERSAL, INC. and SCREEN GEMS-EMI MUSIC INC.
Copyright Renewed
All Rights for the World Controlled and Administered by SONGS OF UNIVERSAL, INC.
All Rights Reserved   Used by Permission

SWAY
(Quien será)

CELLO

English Words by NORMAN GIMBEL
Spanish Words and Music by PABLO BELTRÁN RUIZ
and LUIS DEMETRIO TRACONIS MOLINA

Copyright © 1954 by Editorial Mexicana De Musica Internacional, S.A. and Words West LLC (P.O. Box 15187, Beverly Hills, CA 90209, USA)
Copyright Renewed
All Rights for Editorial Mexicana De Musica Internacional, S.A. Administered by Peer International Corporation
International Copyright Secured   All Rights Reserved

TENNESSEE WALTZ

CELLO

Words and Music by REDD STEWART
and PEE WEE KING

Easy Waltz

Copyright © 1948 Sony/ATV Music Publishing LLC
Copyright Renewed
All Rights Administered by Sony/ATV Music Publishing LLC, 424 Church Street, Suite 1200, Nashville, TN 37219
International Copyright Secured   All Rights Reserved

(THERE IS) NO GREATER LOVE

CELLO

Words by MARTY SYMES
Music by ISHAM JONES

With emotion

Copyright © 1936 (Renewed) by Music Sales Corporation (ASCAP) and Bantam Music Publishing Co.
All Rights for Bantam Music Publishing Co. Administered by WC Music Corp.
International Copyright Secured   All Rights Reserved
Reprinted by Permission

THEY SAY IT'S WONDERFUL

from the Stage Production ANNIE GET YOUR GUN

CELLO

Words and Music by
IRVING BERLIN

© Copyright 1946 by Irving Berlin
Copyright Renewed
International Copyright Secured   All Rights Reserved

THREE TIMES A LADY

CELLO

Words and Music by
LIONEL RICHIE

Copyright © 1978 Jobete Music Co., Inc., Libren Music and Brenda Richie Publishing
All Rights Administered by Sony/ATV Music Publishing LLC, 424 Church Street, Suite 1200, Nashville, TN 37219
International Copyright Secured   All Rights Reserved

TIME TO SAY GOODBYE

CELLO

Words by LUCIO QUARANTOTTO
and FRANK PETERSON
Music by FRANCESCO SARTORI

Copyright © 1995 Sugarmusic Spa - Double Marpot
All Rights Reserved   Used by Permission

(small notes optional)

TRUE COLORS

CELLO

Words and Music by BILLY STEINBERG
and TOM KELLY

Copyright © 1986 Sony/ATV Music Publishing LLC
All Rights Administered by Sony/ATV Music Publishing LLC, 424 Church Street, Suite 1200, Nashville, TN 37219
International Copyright Secured   All Rights Reserved

TRULY

CELLO

Words and Music by
LIONEL RICHIE

Copyright © 1982 by Brockman Music and Brenda Richie Publishing
All Rights Reserved   Used by Permission

UNEXPECTED SONG
from SONG & DANCE

CELLO

Music by ANDREW LLOYD WEBBER
Lyrics by DON BLACK

© Copyright 1978, 1982 Andrew Lloyd Webber licensed to The Really Useful Group Ltd.
International Copyright Secured   All Rights Reserved

WE'VE ONLY JUST BEGUN

Words and Music by ROGER NICHOLS
and PAUL WILLIAMS

Cello

Copyright © 1970 IRVING MUSIC, INC.
Copyright Renewed
All Rights Reserved   Used by Permission

WE'VE GOT TONIGHT

CELLO

Words and Music by
BOB SEGER

Moderately slow

Copyright © 1976, 1978 Gear Publishing Co.
Copyright Renewed

WHAT A WONDERFUL WORLD

CELLO

Words and Music by GEORGE DAVID WEISS
and BOB THIELE

Copyright © 1967 by Range Road Music Inc., Quartet Music and Abilene Music, Inc.
Copyright Renewed
All Rights for Range Road Music Inc. Administered by Round Hill Carlin, LLC
All Rights for Quartet Music Administered by BMG Rights Management (US) LLC
All Rights for Abilene Music, Inc. Administered Worldwide by Imagem Music LLC
International Copyright Secured   All Rights Reserved
Used by Permission

WONDERFUL TONIGHT

Words and Music by
ERIC CLAPTON

CELLO

Copyright © 1977 by Eric Patrick Clapton
Copyright Renewed
International Copyright Secured   All Rights Reserved

YESTER-ME, YESTER-YOU, YESTERDAY

CELLO

Words by RON MILLER
Music by BRYAN WELLS

Moderately

Copyright © 1966 Jobete Music Co., Inc.
Copyright Renewed
All Rights Administered by Sony/ATV Music Publishing LLC, 424 Church Street, Suite 1200, Nashville, TN 37219
International Copyright Secured   All Rights Reserved

YESTERDAY ONCE MORE

CELLO

Words and Music by JOHN BETTIS
and RICHARD CARPENTER

Copyright © 1973 ALMO MUSIC CORP. and HAMMER AND NAILS MUSIC
Copyright Renewed
All Rights Administered by ALMO MUSIC CORP.
All Rights Reserved   Used by Permission

YESTERDAY, WHEN I WAS YOUNG
(Hier Encore)

CELLO

English Lyric by HERBERT KRETZMER
Original French Text and Music by CHARLES AZNAVOUR

© Copyright 1965 (Renewed), 1966 (Renewed) Editions Musicales Charles Aznavour, Paris, France
TRO - Hampshire House Publishing Corp., New York, controls all publication rights for the U.S.A. and Canada
International Copyright Secured
All Rights Reserved Including Public Performance For Profit
Used by Permission

YOU ARE THE SUNSHINE OF MY LIFE

CELLO

Words and Music by
STEVIE WONDER

Copyright © 1972 Jobete Music Co., Inc. and Black Bull Music
Copyright Renewed
All Rights Administered by Sony/ATV Music Publishing LLC, 424 Church Street, Suite 1200, Nashville, TN 37219
International Copyright Secured   All Rights Reserved

YOU'RE THE INSPIRATION

CELLO

Words and Music by PETER CETERA
and DAVID FOSTER

Copyright © 1984 by Universal Music - MGB Songs and Peermusic III, Ltd.
International Copyright Secured   All Rights Reserved

YOUNG AT HEART

from YOUNG AT HEART

Words by CAROLYN LEIGH
Music by JOHNNY RICHARDS

CELLO

© 1954 CHERIO CORP.
© Renewed CHERIO CORP. and JUNE'S TUNES
All Rights Reserved

YOUR SONG

CELLO

Words and Music by ELTON JOHN
and BERNIE TAUPIN

Copyright © 1969 UNIVERSAL/DICK JAMES MUSIC LTD.
Copyright Renewed
All Rights in the United States and Canada Controlled and Administered by UNIVERSAL - SONGS OF POLYGRAM INTERNATIONAL, INC.
All Rights Reserved   Used by Permission